90's HITS

easy playalong *for* flute

WISE PUBLICATIONS
London/New York/Paris/Sydney/Copenhagen/Madrid/Tokyo

Exclusive Distributors:
Music Sales Limited
8/9 Frith Street,
London W1V 5TZ, England.

Music Sales Pty Limited
120 Rothschild Avenue,
Rosebery, NSW 2018,
Australia.

Order No. AM959926
ISBN 0-7119-7802-6
This book © Copyright 2000 by Wise Publications.

Music compiled and arranged by Paul Honey.
Music processed by Enigma Music Production Services.
Cover photography courtesy George Taylor.
Printed in the United Kingdom by
Printwise (Haverhill) Limited, Haverhill, Suffolk.

CD produced by Paul Honey.
Instrumental solos by John Whelan.
All guitars by Arthur Dick.
Engineered by Kester Sims.

Your Guarantee of Quality:
As publishers, we strive to produce every book to
the highest commercial standards.
The music has been freshly engraved and the book
has been carefully designed to minimise awkward page
turns and to make playing from it a real pleasure.
Particular care has been given to specifying acid-free,
neutral-sized paper made from pulps which have not
been elemental chlorine bleached.
This pulp is from farmed sustainable forests and
was produced with special regard for the environment.
Throughout, the printing and binding have been planned
to ensure a sturdy, attractive publication which should
give years of enjoyment.
If your copy fails to meet our high standards,
please inform us and we will gladly replace it.

Music Sales' complete catalogue describes
thousands of titles and is available in full colour
sections by subject, direct from Music Sales Limited.
Please state your areas of interest and send
a cheque/postal order for £1.50 for postage to:
Music Sales Limited, Newmarket Road,
Bury St. Edmunds, Suffolk IP33 3YB.

www.musicsales.com

Fingering Guide

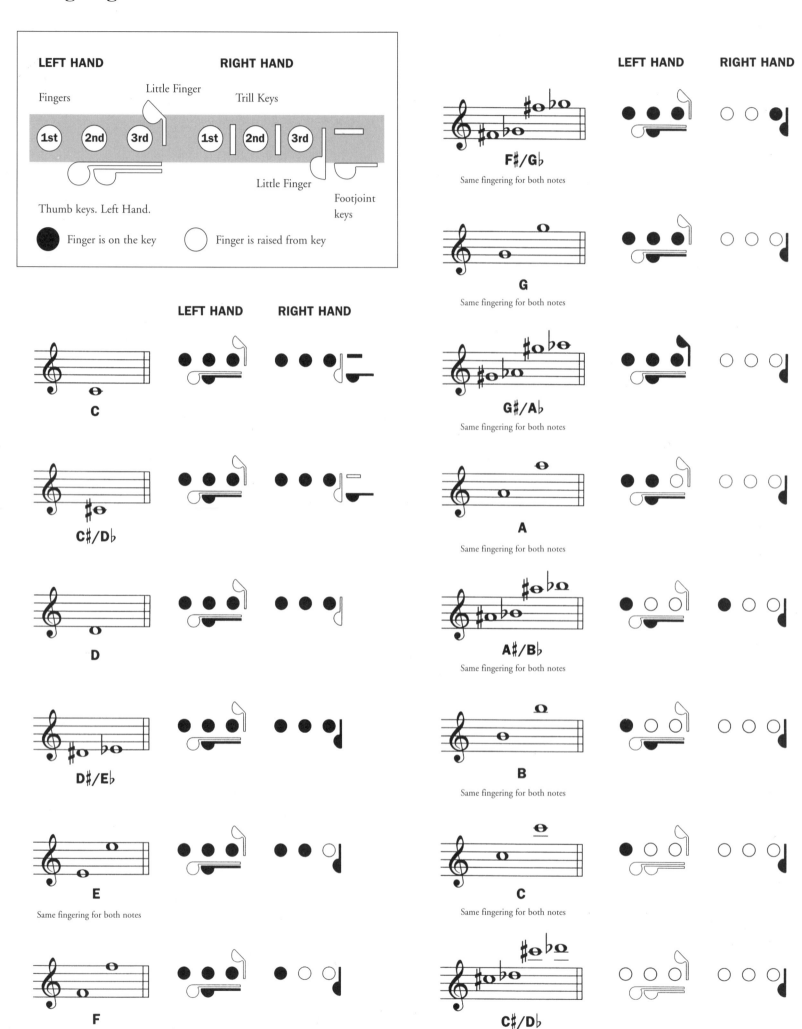

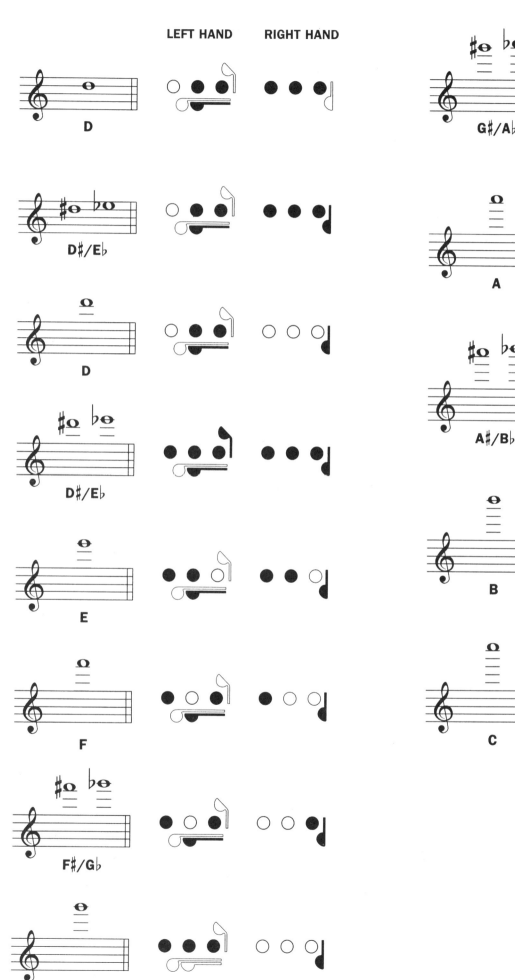
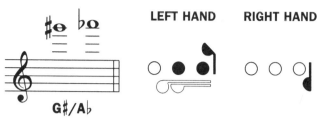
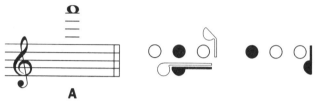
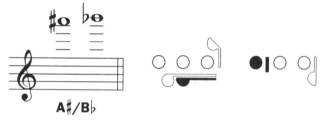
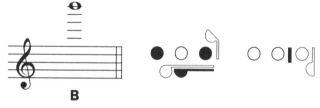
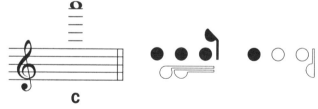

ANGELS

Words & Music by Robbie Williams & Guy Chambers

I sit and wait,— does an

an - gel con - tem - plate my fate, and do they know—

— the pla - ces where we go when we're grey and

old. 'Cos I have been— told that sal -

- va - tion lets their wings un - fold. So when I'm

ly - ing in my bed, thoughts run - ning through my head I

feel that love is dead, I'm lov - ing an - gels in - stead.

1:03
1:40

And through it all_____ she of - fers me_ pro - tec -

- tion, a lot of love and af - fec - tion whe - ther I'm right or

wrong. And down the wa - ter - fall where - ev - er it may

take me I know that life won't break me when I come_ to call

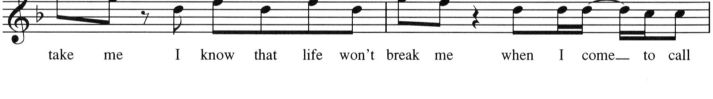
1.

she won't for - sake me, I'm lov - ing an - gels in - stead._

2.

_ And through it all I'm lov - ing an - gels in - stead._

BEAUTIFUL STRANGER

Words & Music by Madonna & William Orbit

HIGH

Words by Paul Tucker
Music by Paul Tucker & Tunde Baiyewu

And we'll won - der_____ how we made it through the

night, at the end of the day re - mem - ber the way we stayed so_close 'til the end,

but re - mem - ber_____ it was me and you. 'Cause we are gon - na

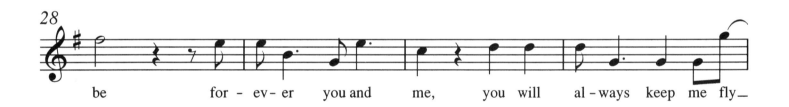
be for - ev - er you and me, you will al - ways keep me fly_

_ ing_high in the sky of love._ 'Cause we are gon-na

be for - ev - er you and me, you will al - ways keep me fly_

_ ing_high in the sky of love._

I HAVE A DREAM

Words & Music by Benny Andersson & Björn Ulvaeus

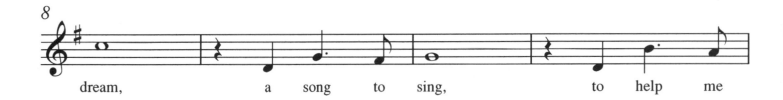

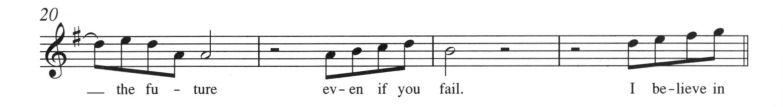

see. I be-lieve in an - gels, when I know the time__ is right__ for__

me, I'll cross the stream, I have a dream. I be-lieve in

an - gels, some-thing good in ev - - 'ry - thing__ I__

see. I be - lieve in an - gels, when I know the

time__ is right__ for__ me, I'll cross the stream, I have a

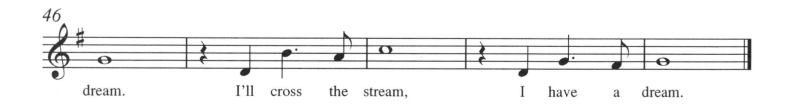

dream. I'll cross the stream, I have a dream.

I WANT IT THAT WAY

Words & Music by Max Martin & Andreas Carlsson

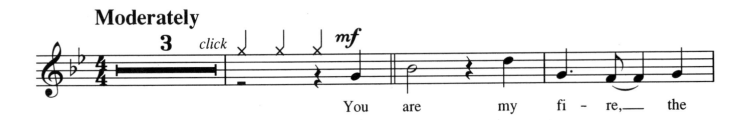

why; I ne-ver wan-na hear you say_____ "I want it that way." Am

1:08

I your fi - re?___ Your one de - si - re?___ Yes I

know it's too late,_ but I want it that way._ Tell me

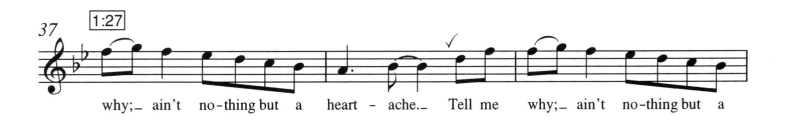

1:27

why;_ ain't no-thing but a heart - ache._ Tell me why;_ ain't no-thing but a

mis - take._ Tell me why; I ne-ver wan-na hear you say_____

"I want it that way."_ I want it that way.

I BELIEVE I CAN FLY

Words & Music by R. Kelly

Now you can own *professional*

when you play all these

for Clarinet, Flute, Alto Saxophone

The *essential* book & CD series...

From Jazz, Blues and Swing to Ballads, Showstoppers, Film and TV Themes, here are all your favourite Chart Hits and more! *Check out* the special editions featuring legends of pop, **Abba** and **The Beatles**.

The Music Book...

Top line arrangements for 10 songs, *plus* a fingering guide for wind instruments.

The CD...

Hear full performance versions of all the songs. Then play along with the recorded accompaniments.

ABBA

Includes:
Dancing Queen
Fernando
Mamma Mia
Waterloo

AM960905 Clarinet
AM960894 Flute
AM960916 Alto Saxophone
AM960927 Violin

BALLADS

Includes:
Candle In The Wind
Imagine
Killing Me Softly With His Song
Wonderful Tonight

AM941787 Clarinet
AM941798 Flute
AM941809 Alto Saxophone

THE BEATLES

Includes:
All You Need Is Love
Hey Jude
Lady Madonna
Yesterday

NO90682 Clarinet
NO90683 Flute
NO90684 Alto Saxophone

CHRISTMAS

Includes:
Frosty The Snowman
Have Yourself A Merry Little
  Christmas
Mary's Boy Child
Winter Wonderland

AM950400 Clarinet
AM950411 Flute
AM950422 Alto Saxophone

have your very backing band...

great melody line arrangements
Tenor Saxophone*, Trumpet* and Violin*

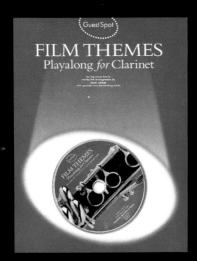

CLASSIC BLUES

Includes:
Fever
Harlem Nocturne
Moonglow
Round Midnight

AM941743 Clarinet
AM941754 Flute
AM941765 Alto Saxophone

CLASSICS

Includes:
Air On The 'G' String - Bach
Jupiter (from The Planets Suite) -
* Holst*
Ode To Joy (Theme from
* Symphony No.9 'Choral') -*
* Beethoven*
Swan Lake (Theme) -
* Tchaikovsky.*

AM955537 Clarinet
AM955548 Flute
AM955560 Violin

FILM THEMES

Includes:
Circle Of Life (The Lion King)
Love Is All Around
* (Four Weddings & A Funeral)*
Moon River
* (Breakfast At Tiffany's)*
You Must Love Me (Evita)

AM941864 Clarinet
AM941875 Flute
AM941886 Alto Saxophone

JAZZ

Includes:
Fly Me To The Moon
Opus One
Satin Doll
Straight No Chaser

AM941700 Clarinet
AM941710 Flute
AM941721 Alto Saxophone

NINETIES HITS

Includes:
Falling Into You (Celine Dion)
Never Ever (All Saints)
Tears In Heaven (Eric Clapton)
2 Become 1 (Spice Girls)

AM952853 Clarinet
AM952864 Flute
AM952875 Alto Saxophone

No.1 HITS

Includes:
A Whiter Shade Of Pale
* (Procol Harum)*
Every Breath You Take
* (The Police)*
No Matter What (Boyzone)
Unchained Melody
* (The Righteous Brothers).*

AM955603 Clarinet
AM955614 Flute
AM955625 Alto Saxophone
AM959530 Violin

SHOWSTOPPERS

Includes:
Big Spender (Sweet Charity)
Bring Him Home (Les Misérables)
I Know Him So Well (Chess)
Somewhere (West Side Story)

AM941820 Clarinet
AM941831 Flute
AM941842 Alto Saxophone

SWING

Includes:
I'm Getting Sentimental
* Over You*
Is You Is Or Is You Ain't
* My Baby?*
Perdido
Tuxedo Junction

AM949377 Clarinet
AM960575 Trumpet
AM949399 Alto Saxophone
AM959618 Tenor Saxophone

TV THEMES

Includes:
Black Adder
Home And Away
London's Burning
Star Trek

AM941908 Clarinet
AM941919 Flute
AM941920 Alto Saxophone

* Selected titles only

Sample the *whole* series of *Guest Spot* with these special double CD bumper compilations...

GUEST SPOT GOLD

Twenty all-time Hit Songs, Showstoppers and Film Themes

Includes:
A Whiter Shade Of Pale (Procol Harum)
Bridge Over Troubled Water
(Simon & Garfunkel)
Don't Cry For Me Argentina (from Evita)
Yesterday (The Beatles)
Where Do I Begin (Theme from Love Story)
Words (Boyzone)
Yesterday (The Beatles)

AM960729 Clarinet
AM960718 Flute
AM960730 Alto Saxophone

GUEST SPOT PLATINUM

Seventeen greatest Chart Hits, Ballads and Film Themes

Includes:
Circle Of Life (from The Lion King)
Candle In The Wind (Elton John)
Dancing Queen (Abba)
Falling Into You (Celine Dion)
I Believe I Can Fly (R. Kelly)
Take My Breath Away (Berlin)
Torn (Natalie Imbruglia

AM960751 Clarinet
AM960740 Flute
AM960762 Alto Saxophone

Available from all good music retailers or,
in case of difficulty, contact:

Music Sales Limited
Newmarket Road, Bury St. Edmunds, Suffolk IP33 3YB.
Telephone 01284 725725 Fax 01284 702592

www.musicsales.com

PUB04626

Love me, love me, say that you love me, fool me, fool me,

go on and fool me, love me, love me, pre - tend that you love me,

leave me, leave me, just say____ that you need me. So I

cry. And I beg for you to

love me, love me, say that you love me, leave me, leave me, just

say that you need me, I can't care a - bout an - y - thing but

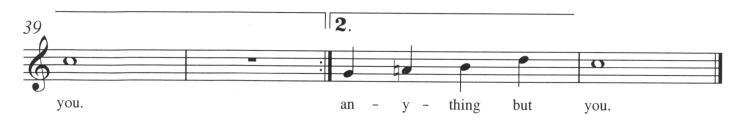

you. an - y - thing but you.

MARVELLOUS

Words & Music by Ian Broudie

Not too fast

Oh— you hope to fit but you're fit

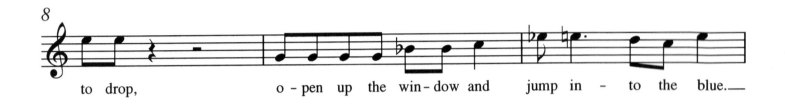

to drop, o - pen up the win-dow and jump in - to the blue.—

———— Things could be mar-vel-lous, things could be

fa - bu-lous. D'you need a push, I'll push— you off,

o - pen up the win-dow and jump in - to the blue.————

Things could be mar-vel-lous soon.— Oh, well these are the

days, this is the life, there'll al-ways be some-thing on your

mind you'll ne-ver quite find. Won't you ev-er make your mind up?

Oh well these are the days and this is the life, there'll al-ways be

some-thing on your mind you'll ne-ver quite find. You used to know but

now you for-got-ten, a sub-ma-rine got stuck to the bot-tom. These are the days so

wake up 'cause this is the time, and you know— I'm— right.

PERFECT MOMENT

Words & Music by James Marr & Wendy Page

Slowly

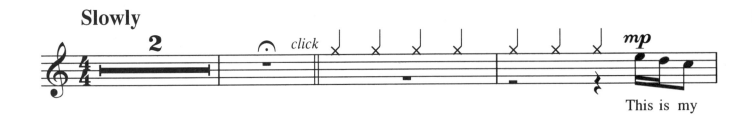

This is my

mo - ment, this is my per - fect mo - ment with___ you.

This is what God meant, this is my per - fect mo - ment with_

_ you. Wish I could freeze this space in

time, the way that I feel___ for you in - side._____ This is my

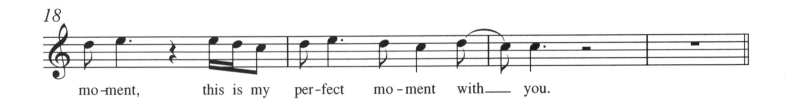

mo - ment, this is my per - fect mo - ment with___ you.

Tell me you love me, when you—leave, you're more than a sha-dow,

that's what I—— be lieve. You take me to pla-ces I ne-ver thought I'd see.——

Min-ute by min-ute you're the world to me.— I wish I could frame the look in your

eyes, the way that I feel, for you in - side.———— This is my

mo-ment, this is my per-fect mo-ment with— you.— This is my

mo-ment, this is my per-fect mo-ment with— you.—

SEARCH FOR THE HERO

Words & Music by Mike Pickering & Paul Heard

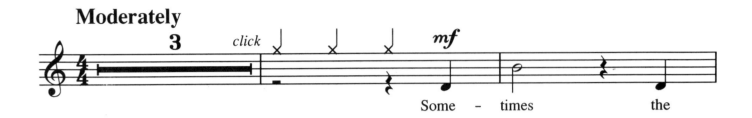

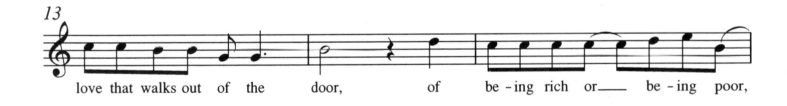

then that faith ar-rives, to make you feel at least a - live,___ and that's

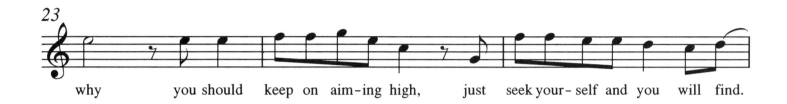
why you should keep on aim-ing high, just seek your-self and you will find.

f

1:04
1:24

___ You've got to search for the rea - son in - side your-self,

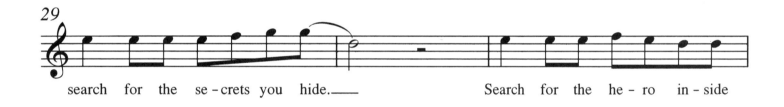
search for the se -crets you hide.___ Search for the he - ro in - side

1.

your - self, un – til you find the key to your

2.

life. You've got to - til you find the key to your life.

SO YOUNG

Words & Music by Andrea Corr, Caroline Corr, Sharon Corr & Jim Corr

And when to - mor - row comes, we can do it all a - gain.

Yeah we are so young now, we are so young, so young now.

And when to - mor - row comes we'll just do it all a - gain.

1:28

mf

Yeah, yeah, yeah, yeah,

yeah. Yeah, yeah, yeah, yeah,

yeah. Yeah, yeah, yeah, yeah, yeah.

Yeah, yeah, yeah, yeah, yeah.

STOP

Words & Music by Victoria Aadams, Emma Bunton, Melanie Brown,
Melanie Chisholm, Geri Halliwell, Andy Watkins & Paul Wilson

Brightly

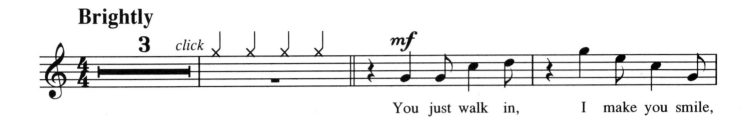

You just walk in, I make you smile,

it's cool but you don't ev - en know me.— You take an inch,

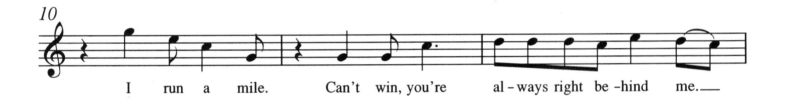

I run a mile. Can't win, you're al - ways right be -hind me.—

And we know that you could go and find some oth - er, take or leave it or just

don't ev - en both - er.— Caught in a craze, it's just a phase, or will this

be a-round for ev - er?___ Don't you know it's go-in' too fast,

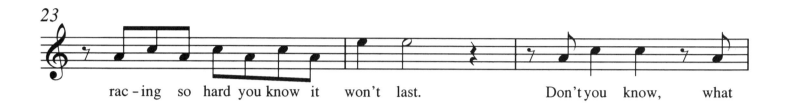

rac-ing so hard you know it won't last. Don't you know, what

cresc.

can't you see, Slow it down, read the sign, so you know just where you're go - in'.

Stop right now, thank you ve-ry much. I need some-bo-dy with a

hu - man touch._____ Hey you, al-ways on the run. Got-ta

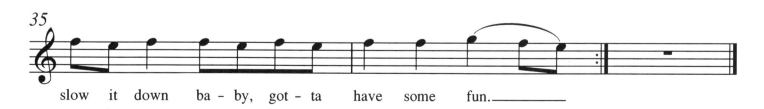

slow it down ba - by, got-ta have some fun._____

NO MATTER WHAT

Words by Jim Steinman
Music by Andrew Lloyd Webber

7/02 (44729)

B flat instruments edition

Sixty Christmas favourites
for B flat instruments including Clarinet
Trumpet, Cornet and Tenor Sax

Selected and arranged by Colin Hand

Kevin
Mayhew

We hope you enjoy *All the carols you've ever wanted to play* (B♭ instruments).
Further copies are available from your local music shop.

In case of difficulty, please contact the publisher direct:

The Sales Department
KEVIN MAYHEW LTD
Rattlesden
Bury St Edmunds
Suffolk IP30 0SZ

Phone 0449 737978
Fax 0449 737834

Please ask for our complete catalogue of outstanding Instrumental Music.

Acknowledgements

The publishers wish to express their gratitude to Oxford University Press for
permission to use the following copyright material in this book:

Gloucestershire Wassail; hymn tune Hermitage (*Love came down at Christmas*)
from *Songs of Praise;* hymn tune Forest Green (*O little town of Bethlehem*)
from the *English Hymnal.*

All other material is copyright Kevin Mayhew Ltd.

First published in Great Britain in 1993 by Kevin Mayhew Ltd.

© Copyright 1993 Kevin Mayhew Ltd.

ISBN 0 86209 455 0

Cover illustration by Arthur Baker.
Cover design by Graham Johnstone.
Music selected and arranged by Colin Hand.
Music Setting: Louise Hill.

Printed and bound in Great Britain.

Contents

HARK, THE HERALD ANGELS SING

Felix Mendelssohn

At a moderate pace

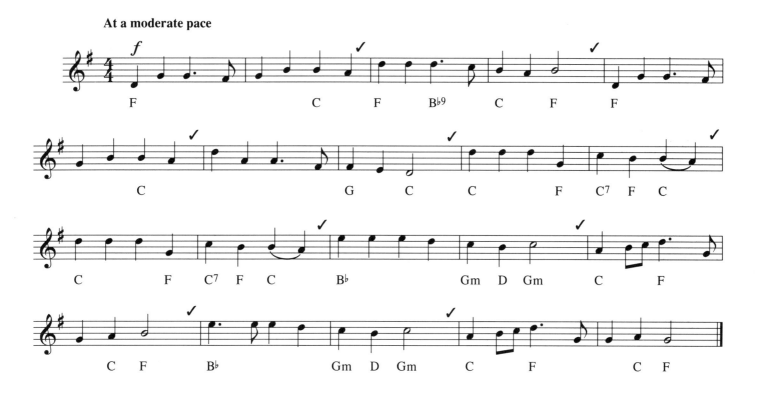

GLOUCESTERSHIRE WASSAIL

Traditional English Melody

Quite quickly

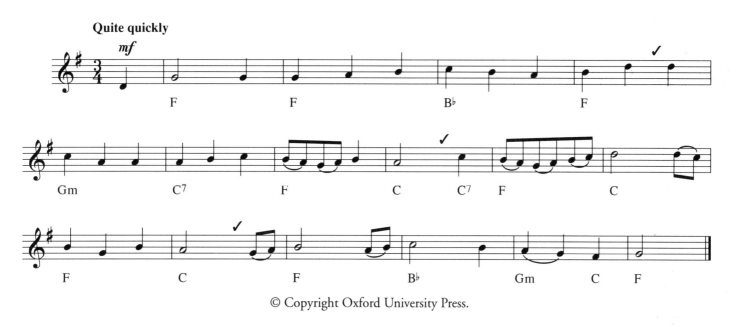

LOVE CAME DOWN AT CHRISTMAS
R.O. Morris

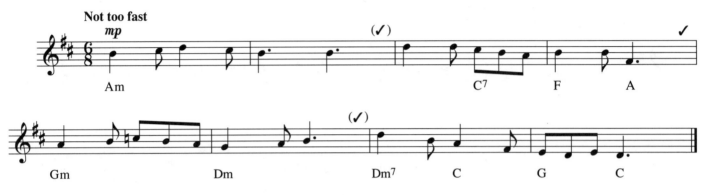

BLESSED BE THAT MAID MARY
Traditional English Melody

CHILD IN THE MANGER
Old Gaelic Melody

JINGLE BELLS
James Pierpont

INFANT HOLY, INFANT LOWLY
Traditional Polish Melody

A VIRGIN MOST PURE

Traditional English Melody

UNTO US IS BORN A SON

16th Century Melody

IN THE BLEAK MIDWINTER

Gustav Holst

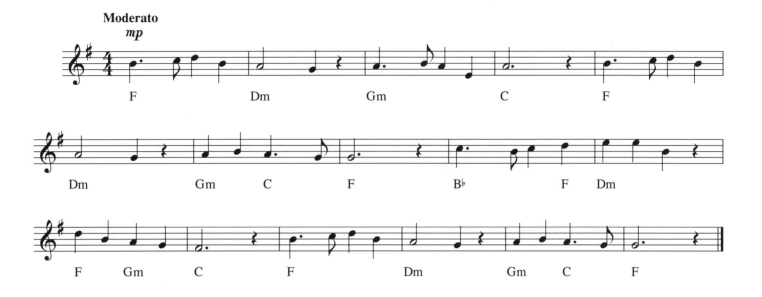

JOSEPH DEAREST, JOSEPH MINE

Traditional German Melody

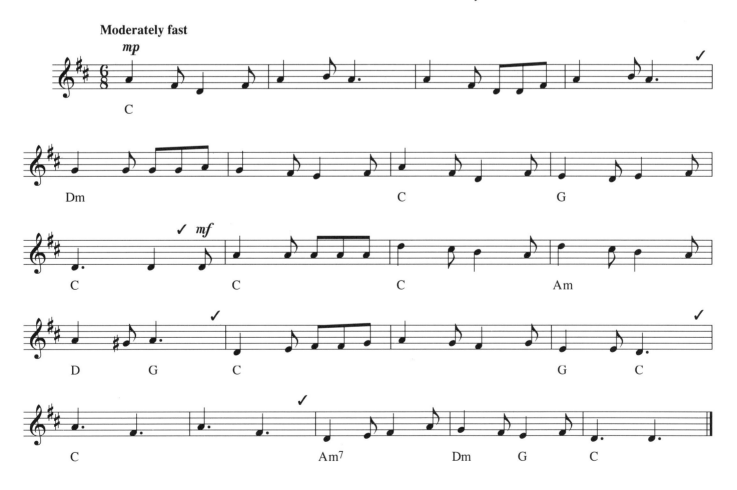

DING DONG! MERRILY ON HIGH

Traditional French Melody

SEE AMID THE WINTER'S SNOW

John Goss

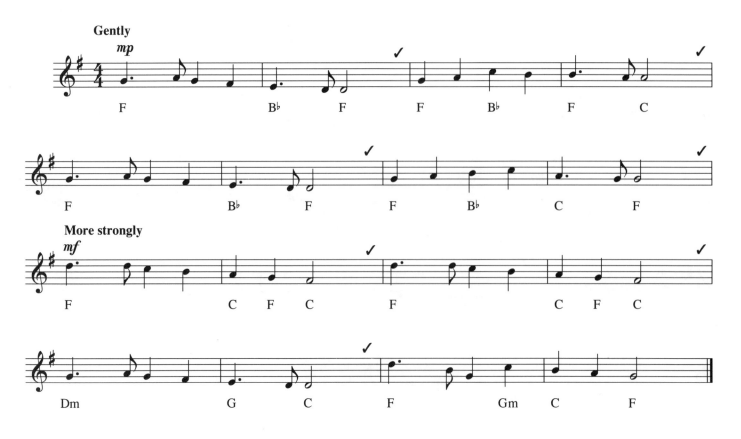

MARY HAD A BABY
Traditional West Indian Melody

I SAW THREE SHIPS
Traditional English Melody

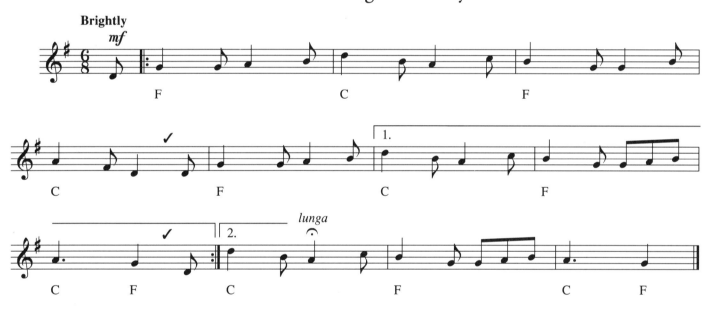

WHILE SHEPHERDS WATCHED
16th Century Melody

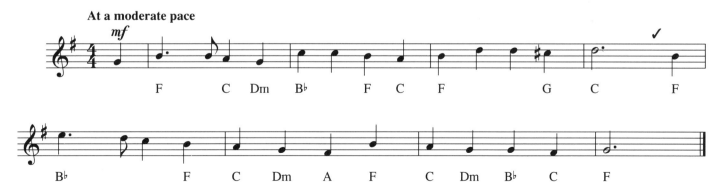

THE SANS DAY CAROL

Traditional English Melody

O LITTLE TOWN OF BETHLEHEM (1)

Traditional English Melody

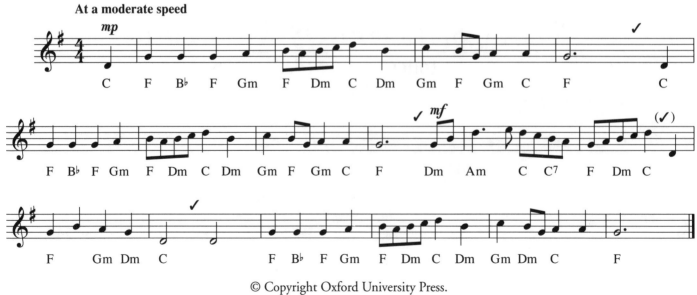

O LITTLE TOWN OF BETHLEHEM (2)

Henry Walford Davies

O LITTLE ONE SWEET

Traditional German Melody

PATAPAN
Traditional French Melody

GO TELL IT ON THE MOUNTAIN
Traditional English Melody

GOD REST YOU MERRY, GENTLEMEN

Traditional English Melody

SUSSEX CAROL

Traditional English Melody

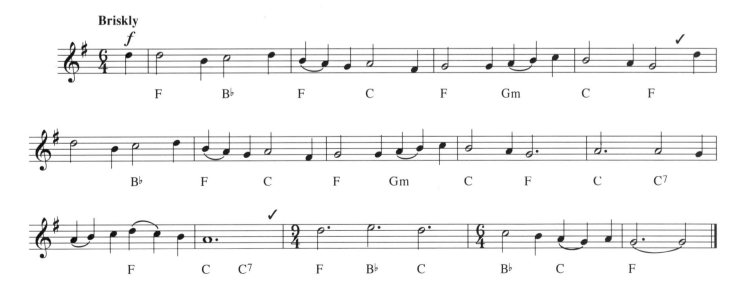

WE THREE KINGS

John Henry Hopkins

RISE UP, SHEPHERD, AND FOLLOW

American Spiritual

SILENT NIGHT
Franz Grüber

ZITHER CAROL
Traditional Czech Melody

GREEN GROW'TH THE HOLLY
Attributed to Henry VIII

THE VIRGIN MARY HAD A BABY BOY

Traditional West Indian Melody

A GREAT AND MIGHTY WONDER

Old German Melody

THE ANGEL GABRIEL

Basque Folk Melody

LORD JESUS HATH A GARDEN

Dutch Melody

THE BOAR'S HEAD CAROL

Traditional English Melody

THE FIRST NOWELL

Traditional English Melody

ANGELS FROM THE REALMS OF GLORY
Traditional French Melody

ROCKING
Traditional Czech Melody

THE BELLMAN'S CAROL
Traditional English Melody

COVENTRY CAROL
15th Century Melody

THE MERRY, MERRY MORN
Traditional English Melody

REJOICE AND BE MERRY
Traditional English Melody

AS I WENT TO BETHLEHEM
Traditional English Melody

PAST THREE O'CLOCK
Traditional English Melody

THE SEVEN JOYS OF MARY

Traditional English Melody

THREE KINGS FROM PERSIAN LANDS AFAR

Peter Cornelius

AWAY IN A MANGER

William James Kirkpatrick

THE BIRD'S CAROL

Traditional Czech Carol

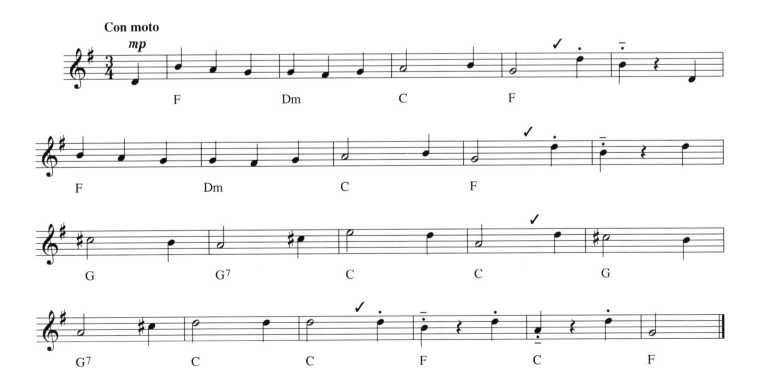

GOOD KING WENCESLAS

Traditional English Melody

THIS ENDRIS NIGHT

Old English Melody

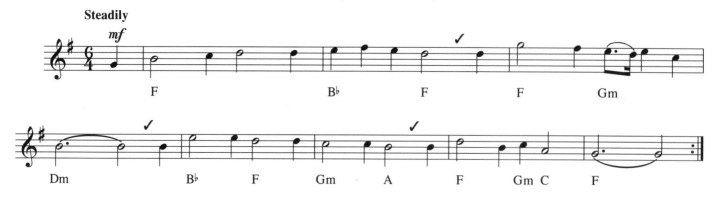

THE SHEPHERDS' CAROL

Traditional German Melody

CHRISTIANS AWAKE

John Wainwright

THE HOLLY AND THE IVY

Traditional English Melody

IN DULCI JUBILO

16th Century Melody

ONCE IN ROYAL DAVID'S CITY

Henry John Gauntlett

IL EST NÉ

Traditional French Melody

HERE WE COME A-WASSAILING

Traditional English Melody

UP! GOOD CHRISTIAN FOLK

16th Century Melody

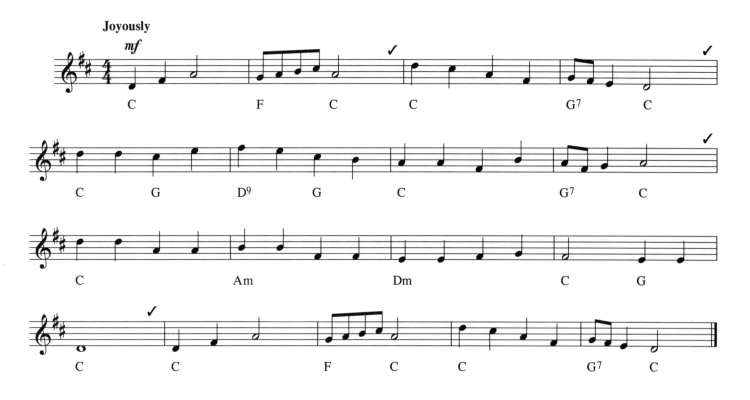

IT CAME UPON THE MIDNIGHT CLEAR

Traditional English Melody

WE WISH YOU A MERRY CHRISTMAS

Traditional English Melody

O COME, ALL YE FAITHFUL

John Francis Wade

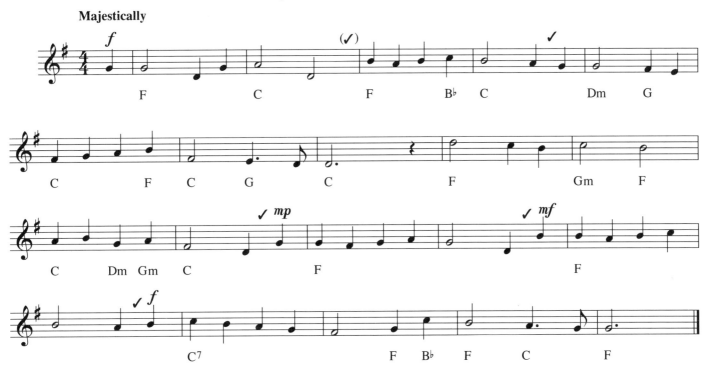